Savvy

Girlology

BODY PRO

Facts and figures
about bad hair days,
blemishes and being healthy

Erin Falligant

raintree

a Capstone company — publishers for children

Raintree is an imprint of Capstone Global Library Limited, a company incorporated in England and Wales having its registered office at 264 Banbury Road, Oxford, OX2 7DY – Registered company number: 6695582

www.raintree.co.uk myorders@raintree.co.uk

Text © 2018 Capstone Global Library Limited 2018
The moral rights of the proprietor have been asserted.

Edited by Mandy Robbins
Designed by Kayla Rossow
Original illustrations © Capstone Global Library Limited 2018
Picture research by Jo Miller
Production by Kathy McColley
Originated by Capstone Global Library Ltd Printed and bound in India

ISBN 978 1 4747 4810 0
22 21 20 19 18
10 9 8 7 6 5 4 3 2 1

British Library Cataloguing in Publication Data
A full catalogue record for this book is available from the British Library.

Acknowledgements
We would like to thank the following for permission to reproduce photographs:
Getty Images: Hulton Archive/Stringer, 15bl; Shutterstock: aarrows, 22bl, Africa Studio, 21bl, Akkalak Aiempradit, 11tr, Aleks Melnik, 25bl, 25br, amelissimo, 20r, Anastacia Trapeznikova, 20l, Anastasiia Skorobogatova, 21ml, AnaV, 13bl, Andy Dean Photography, 23r, Ann Haritonenko, 23ml, Annie Dove, 20l, asharkyu, 11mr, bigacis, 21tm, Binh Thanh Bui, 19tm, 19tr, borsvelka, 20l, Brainsil, 10, Bryan Solomon, 7, Catherine Glazkova, 27bm, chronicler, 20r, curiosity, 20l, designer_an, 31t, Designua, 12bl, Diana Taliun, 19br, Evikka, 21tr, Flaffy, 21mr, Gelpi, 25t, ifong, 18t, ImageFlow, 28, iordani, 30, Iraida-art, 24, 25r, Jane_Lane, 27br, JeniFoto, 21br, Josep Curto, 19bl, Kamieshkova, 20r, KeKi Chulaket, 11b, Kencana Studio, 20tr, KucherAV, 21tl, Lermot, 20r, LynxVector, 14, MaeManee, 29, MANDY GODBEHEAR, 4, MaraZe, 19bm, Marushchak Olha, 22t, mhatzapa, 20r, Michal Sanca, 22br, nikiteev_konstantin, 16, Olga_Angelloz, 31b, pathdoc, 17, pukach, 13br, Rohappy, 23l, Romariolen, 21bm, Samuel Borges Photography, 23m, Skobrik, 15tr, Sonya illustration, 12t, stereoliar, 5, 13tl, swinner, 21mr, Syda Productions, 26, Syrytsyna Tetiana, 27t, szefei, 23mr, Tatiana Ka, 27bl, Tim UR, 19tl, Vixit, 20r, Vladimir Gjorgiev, 9tl, wavebreakmedia, 18b

Design Elements
Capstone Studio: Karon Dubke; Shutterstock: AD Hunter, Alena Ohneva, Alsou Shakurova, Angie Makes, Antun Hirsman, AnyRama, Brian Chase, Dzha33, graphixmania, Icons vector, krasivo, Macrovector, Mariam27, MicroOne, Pavel K, Pushistaja, Yulia Yemelianova

Printed and bound in India.

CONTENTS

Chapter 1

KNOW YOUR BODY

How fast do your hair and nails grow? What percentage of girls struggle with spots? How much sleep do you *really* need at night? Get the facts and figures about your body, and learn how other girls view and care for themselves too. Knowing the numbers can help you feel more confident about your growing, changing body. It will also help you know what to expect *next*.

age 8:
Most girls begin puberty between the ages of 8 and 13.

age 9:
50% of girls aged 9 to 12 think they're overweight, but only 15% actually are.

age 10:
The average girl begins her growth spurt at age 10. Girls can grow 9 centimetres (3.5 inches) per year during puberty.

age 11:
76% of 11-year-olds do NOT get enough exercise every day.

The average girl gets her first bra at the age of 11½.

age 12:
71% of parents think it's okay for a 12-year-old girl to begin shaving her legs.

The average girl starts her period at the age of 12.

age 13:
71% of 13-year-olds do NOT get enough sleep on school nights.

50% of girls wear make-up between the ages of 11 and 13 years old.

age 14:
15% of 14- to 17-year-olds wear contact lenses.

An active 14-year-old needs 2400 calories a day.

HAIR, HERE AND THERE

You cut it, you clip it, you brush it and you plait it. When hair starts to grow in new places, you might even pluck and shave it. Get all the hairy details here.

100,000:
approximate number of hairs on your head

2 to 6:
how many years each hair "lives" on your head

50 to 100:
strands that fall out every day

0.04 to 0.1 millimetre:
the thickness of a strand of hair

1.3 centimetres:
your hair's average growth each month

1.5 metres:
how long your hair could grow if you never cut it

HOW OFTEN SHOULD YOU SHAMPOO?
Shampooing too often can dry out your hair and scalp. How often is enough for you? Answer these questions to find out.

Want to shower on non-shampoo days?
Just rinse your hair with water and use conditioner.
Presto – healthier hair!

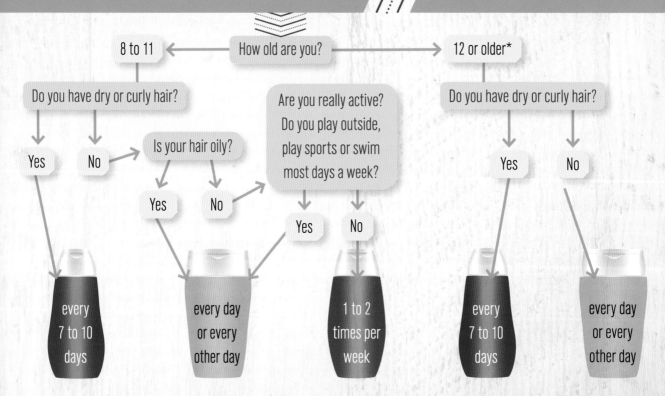

How old are you?

8 to 11

Do you have dry or curly hair?

Yes → every 7 to 10 days

No → Is your hair oily?
- Yes → every day or every other day
- No →

Are you really active? Do you play outside, play sports or swim most days a week?
- Yes → every day or every other day
- No → 1 to 2 times per week

12 or older*

Do you have dry or curly hair?
- Yes → every 7 to 10 days
- No → every day or every other day

*If you're not quite 12 but have started puberty, follow the tips for ages 12 and older.

HAIR ON LEGS AND UNDERARMS

Puberty may cause the hair on your legs to get darker and thicker. You'll grow hair under your arms too. Some girls and women choose to shave it. Others leave it. Talk to your parents and decide what's right for you.

WHEN TO START SHAVING LEGS? PARENTS SAY:

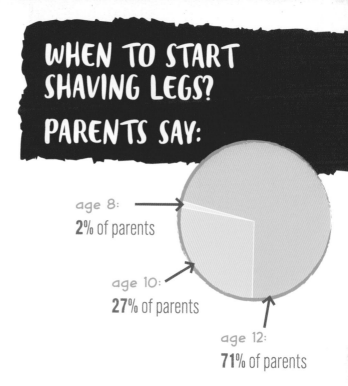

age 8:
2% of parents

age 10:
27% of parents

age 12:
71% of parents

FACIAL HAIR

Some girls worry about thick eyebrows or the darkening of hair above their upper lip. Shaving isn't usually the best removal option for facial hair. When you shave off the soft tip, hair can feel coarse as it grows back. Tweezing and waxing, which remove hair at the root, last longer.

How often you need to:							
tweeze	3 to 8 weeks						
wax	3 to 6 weeks						
shave	1 to 3 days						
week	1	2	3	4	5	6	7	8

INGROWN HAIR

An ingrown hair is one that curls around and grows back into your skin. It can cause an itchy or painful red bump. Shaving, waxing and tweezing can all cause ingrown hairs. Follow a parent or guardian's advice for the safest way to remove hair.

THE DOWNSIDES?

Tweezing and waxing can be painful and expensive. Most parents want girls to wait until they're at least 14.

When is it okay for girls to start tweezing or waxing?

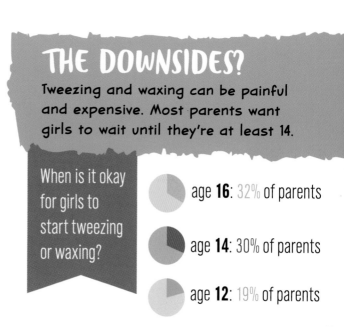

age **16**: 32% of parents

age **14**: 30% of parents

age **12**: 19% of parents

HANDS AND NAILS

Your hands and nails say a lot about you. But it takes time to care for them – and to break that pesky nail-biting habit.

SUDS UP

Handwashing is the most important way to prevent spreading germs, illness, and infection. But only...

58% of teen girls and **48**% of teen boys wash their hands after using the toilet.

Kids who wash their hands at least 4 times a day take. . .

51% fewer sick days due to stomach illness.

24% fewer sick days from school due to colds and the flu.

20 seconds: the amount of time you should spend washing your hands to make sure they're really clean.

GROWING YOUR NAILS

Fingernails grow faster than toenails, especially on your dominant hand. If you're right handed, the nails on your right hand grow faster! And all nails grow faster in the summer than in the winter.

3.5: how many millimetres fingernails grow every month

1: the number of millimetres toenails grow every month

6: the number of months it might take to grow back a fingernail if you lost one in an injury

18: how many months it might take to grow back a lost toenail

HEALTHY NAILS = HEALTHY BODY

Changes in your nails could be a sign of other health problems. Tell your parents or your doctor if:

- you notice a dark streak under a nail
- your nails' natural colour changes
- your nails get thicker or thinner
- the skin swells around a nail

NAIL NIBBLERS

50% of children between the ages of 10 and 18 bite their nails.

30 is the age when most people outgrow the habit.

TO PAINT OR NOT TO PAINT?

Nail varnish and varnish remover can be hard on your nails.

3 the number of chemicals that make up the "toxic trio" in many nail varnishes.

Did you know?
Nail varnish originates from China and was first used around 5,000 years ago! It was made using beeswax, egg whites and vegetable dyes.

If you polish your nails, do it in a well-ventilated space. Look for water-based varnishes. And choose a moisturizing varnish remover or one without acetone, a chemical that dries out nails.

10 out of 12
nail varnishes labelled as being "toxin free" that actually contain toxic chemicals.

EYES, EARS AND MOUTH

Are you getting contact lenses? Already wearing braces?
Thinking about piercing your ears? You're not alone!

CHANGING EYES

As you get older, chances increase that you'll need a prescription to correct your vision. One study showed that nearly a third of teens wear glasses or contacts lenses.

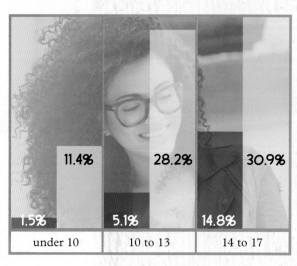

contact
lenses

prescription
eyeglasses

	11.4%	28.2%	30.9%
1.5%		5.1%	14.8%
under 10		10 to 13	14 to 17

WANT TO TRY CONTACT LENSES?

3 MILLION
people in the UK wear contact lenses.

5%
of people under 18 wear contact lenses.

12 or 13
is how old most experts think kids should be before they get contacts.

WHY WAIT? BECAUSE...

- **68%** of contact lens wearers don't correctly follow the care instructions given to them.

- About **25%** of children's A&E visits every year are related to eye infections or injuries caused by contact lenses.

There are good reasons to wear contact lenses, but always follow your eye doctor's instructions for changing and cleaning them.

PIERCED EARS

Did you know that 7 is the average age that girls in the UK have their ears pierced? If you have pierced ears or are thinking of getting them pierced, you need to know how to care for them properly.

CARING FOR PIERCED EARS

1 how many times a day you should wash your pierced ears with soap and water

2 how many times a day you should apply alcohol with a cotton wool ball

3 how many times a day you should gently twist the studs in your ears

6 the number of weeks you should leave studs in, even at night, until your ears are completely healed

Note: If your ears feel sore, look red or puffy, or ooze liquid, ask your doctor to check them for infection.

BRACES
Getting braces? Join the club!

• **Around 200,000** people start orthodontic treatment every year in the UK.

• **9 to 14:** the age range when most children get braces

• **2 years:** the average length of time braces are worn

• **3 tips for surviving braces:**
  • Brush teeth after every snack or meal.
  • Floss every night. Ask your orthodontist to show you tricks for getting above the brace's brackets.
  • Steer clear of hard foods or sticky foods that can break or loosen braces.

SKIN SKILLS

Struggling with acne? Experimenting with make-up? Many other girls are too. Here are some stats on the skin you're in.

ABOUT ACNE

8 in 10:
tweens and teens have acne

14 to 17:
age you're most likely to get acne

1 to 2:
how many times you should wash your face every day

3 fictions:
- Chocolate causes acne. (It doesn't.)
- Greasy foods cause acne. (They don't.)
- Stress causes acne. (It doesn't either.)

3 facts:
- Changes in hormones during puberty can cause acne.
- Acne may be hereditary. (If your parents had acne, you might too.)
- Greasy make-up can lead to acne. Always wash it off at night with a gentle cleanser.

HOW ACNE DEVELOPS

A spot forms when a healthy pore becomes a clogged pore. Bacteria spreads within the gland beneath the skin.

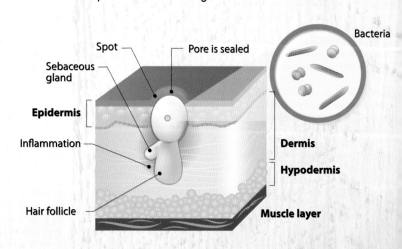

Bacteria

Spot

Pore is sealed

Sebaceous gland

Epidermis

Inflammation

Dermis

Hypodermis

Hair follicle

Muscle layer

12

MAKE-UP? MAYBE, MAYBE NOT

3 out of 5 girls
ages 8 to 18 wear make-up.

WHEN DID THEY START?

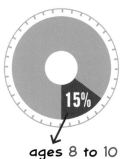

15%
ages 8 to 10

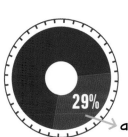

29%
ages 11 to 13

ages 14 to 16
50%

TOP MAKE-UP PICKS FOR TWEENS?

15% wear eyeliner

15% wear lipstick

18% wear mascara

OF THE GIRLS WHO WEAR MAKE-UP...

- **80%** feel fine about themselves when they don't wear it, and...
- **73%** feel fine leaving the house without it.
- **5%** say going without make-up makes them feel more attractive.

27/2/12:

The date when the first Barefaced & Beautiful, Within and Without campaign kicked off. It encouraged girls and women to go without make-up for a day, and to post selfies on social media. Barefaced can be beautiful!

Celebrities such as Alicia Keys and Alessia Cara have embraced a make-up-free lifestyle. Many of their fans have done the same.

BREASTS AND BRAS

Like the rest of your body during puberty, breasts grow too. Some girls worry their breasts are growing too quickly. Others worry they're not growing quickly enough. Breast development takes time. In the meantime, find a bra that fits.

10

10 to 11:
the age when most girls' breasts begin to develop (But it can start as early as age 7 or as late as age 13.)

11

11 to 12:
the average age that a girl gets her first bra

12

12 to 13:
the average age that a girl gets a bra with a cup size

13

UNEVEN BREASTS?

Breasts often grow at different rates during puberty. The difference in size will even out as you get older. But more than **50%** of adult women have some kind of breast asymmetry. That means their breasts don't match exactly. And it's perfectly normal!

BRA BASICS

cups

bra straps

underwire

bra bands

bra hooks

Don't know what size you are? Do the maths:

1. Use a tape measure to measure your ribcage, just under your breasts.

2. Add 5 inches.

3. If you get an odd number, (such as 29, 31 or 33), subtract 1 to round down to the nearest even number, (such as 28, 30, or 32). Bras usually stretch over time. The total is your band size.

4. Measure across the fullest part of your breasts. Subtract your band size from this number. The answer to this equation is your cup size:

$$0'' = AA \qquad 1'' = A \qquad 2'' = B$$

$$3'' = C \qquad 4'' = D$$

5. Put your band size together with your cup size to get your bra size (such as 32A).

8 out of 10
women wear bras that don't fit!

Need help?
Ask for it! An older sister, your mum or aunty, or even a sales assistant in the lingerie department can help you find your best fit.

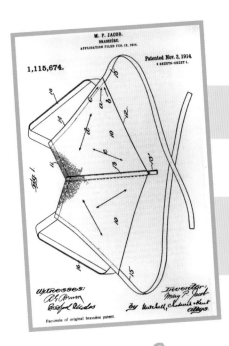

THE FIRST BRA - EVER!

1914: when the first modern bra was invented

19: Mary Phelps Jacob's age when she invented the bra

2: the number of handkerchiefs she sewed together to create the bra

THE FACTS. PERIOD.

Getting your period can be one of the most exciting – and scariest – parts of puberty. But the more you know in advance, the less scary it'll be. Your body already knows what to do, and every woman you know has gone through it too.

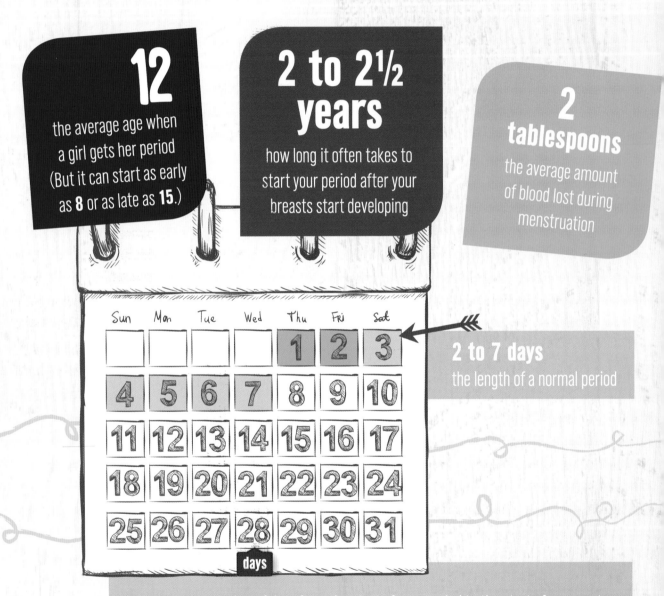

12
the average age when a girl gets her period (But it can start as early as **8** or as late as **15**.)

2 to 2½ years
how long it often takes to start your period after your breasts start developing

2 tablespoons
the average amount of blood lost during menstruation

2 to 7 days
the length of a normal period

Sun	Mon	Tue	Wed	Thu	Fri	Sat
				1	2	3
4	5	6	7	8	9	10
11	12	13	14	15	16	17
18	19	20	21	22	23	24
25	26	27	28	29	30	31

days

The average number of days from the start of your period to the start of your next one. But menstrual cycles can last anywhere from **21 to 45 days**, especially in the first year or two. Track yours on a calendar or with an app, and you'll start to see what's normal for you.

PERIOD MYTHS: TRUE OR FALSE?

1. Period blood differs from the rest of your blood.

2. Certain foods may make cramps worse.

3. You shouldn't exercise during your period.

4. It can take six months or more for a young woman's period to become regular.

✗ 1. FALSE – Blood is the same no matter what part of your body it's from.
✓ 2. TRUE – Avoid the following foods to try to lessen period cramps: dairy, sugar, white grains, fatty meat and salty foods.
✗ 3. FALSE – Exercise may actually boost your mood and lessen cramping.
✓ 4. TRUE – Periods can be irregular for the first year a girl has her cycle.

WHAT TO USE?

Some girls use only pads. Other girls use pads when they sleep and tampons during the day. Some prefer menstrual cups. Whatever product you use, remember to change it regularly to lower your risk of infection. Special absorbent underwear is a new product that may be the right choice for you.

Product	Pros	Cons
Pads	-Easy to use -Many options available for coverage and light to heavy flow	-Can be bulky and/or uncomfortable -May leak -May not stay in place while exercising or sleeping
Tampons	-Discreet to carry -No external mess -Able to exercise and swim comfortably	-Can be tricky or intimidating to learn to use -Minor possibility of infection
Menstrual cups	-Can be worn up to 12 hours with no leakage -Reusable cups are environmentally friendly.	-Tricky to learn to use -Reusable cups are messy to clean.
Absorbent underwear	-One pair lasts 25 to 30 washes -May save you money over time -Environmentally friendly	-Expensive initial purchase -Washing can be tricky and messy -You need more than one pair -May need to be used with a tampon or menstrual cup

Chapter 2

NUTRITION: WHAT YOU MIGHT BE MISSING

To keep your body healthy as it changes and grows, you need to fuel up with the right foods. You know about the major food groups. But do you know if you're getting enough foods from each?

FOOD GROUPS

This food pie chart shows the relative amounts of the different food groups that you should be eating.

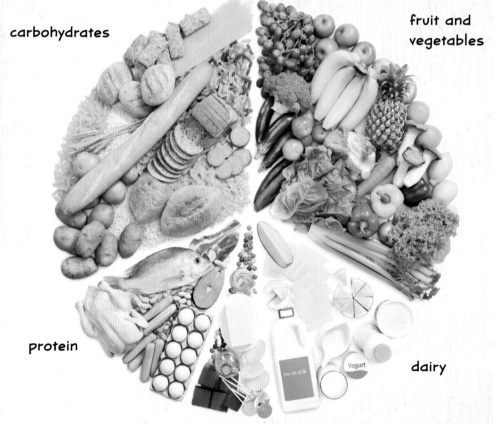

carbohydrates

fruit and vegetables

protein

dairy

treats

WHAT'S A SERVING?

If you're like most girls, you need at least one more serving of fruit and veggies a day – plus another serving of dairy. But what does a "serving" look like?

ONE SERVING

of fruit or veggies looks like this. . .

or this. . .

1 apple

6 baby carrots

or this.

75 g of broccoli

Need a serving of dairy?

Try this. . .

or this. . .

1 glass of milk

1 pot of yoghurt

or this.

1 piece of string cheese

Note: Milk and yoghurt should be 225 ml servings.

YOUR BODY ON BREAKFAST

You've heard that it's the most important meal of the day. So why do so many people skip it? You may not be a morning person, but giving yourself time for breakfast will do your body good.

32%
of adolescents
don't eat
breakfast

10 REASONS NOT TO MISS BREAKFAST

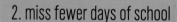
Kids who eat a healthy breakfast may...

1. be more punctual

2. miss fewer days of school

3. have a more positive mood

4. pay attention more easily at school

5. find it easier to memorize information

6. get along more easily with peers
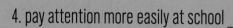

7. perform better in maths and reading

8. get better test results

9. make more nutritious food choices all day long

10. stay at a healthier weight

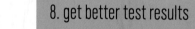
... than kids who don't.

PICK 3 OUT OF 5

The best breakfast includes at least 3 out of 5 food groups. Get creative with your combos, even when you're grabbing breakfast on the go.

1 Grain +

1 small bowl of porridge, 1 piece of bread or toast, 1 small bowl of cereal

1 Fruit or Vegetable +

½ apple, a handful of berries, 1 banana

1 Dairy or Protein =

1 tablespoon of peanut butter, 1 pot of yoghurt, 1 glass of milk

A better breakfast!

Chapter 3

BODIES IN THE MEDIA

Do you ever compare your body to the models you see on TV or in magazines? Most girls do. But don't be fooled by what you see.

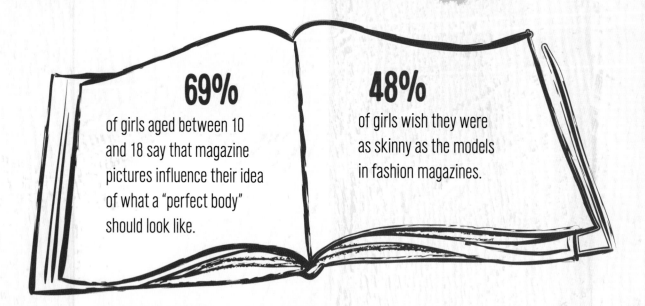

69%

of girls aged between 10 and 18 say that magazine pictures influence their idea of what a "perfect body" should look like.

48%

of girls wish they were as skinny as the models in fashion magazines.

WHAT'S REALISTIC?

Take a look at how a model's body compares to *most* women's bodies. Remember that healthy bodies come in a wide variety of shapes and sizes.

the average woman in the UK

5' 3" tall
11 stone

the average UK model

5' 11" tall
8.4 stone

2% the number of women who have a body like the ones shown in magazines

98% the number of women who DON'T

DIGITAL MAGIC

Even most fashion models don't have the bodies you see in ads – their photographs are digitally edited to make them look perfect.

Want to change what you see in the media? You're not alone.

81% of girls would rather see true-to-life photos of models instead of touched-up, photo-edited ones.

So speak up and say so! Email or write to your favourite magazines and tell them to show *real* women and girls – like you.

Chapter 4

TREAT YOUR BODY RIGHT

Why exercise? Not only does it burn calories to keep your body at a healthy weight, but it makes you feel good too.

THE MORE ACTIVE YOU ARE, THE MORE CALORIES YOU NEED.

See for yourself. An active 9-year-old needs just as many calories every day as an idle 14-year-old.

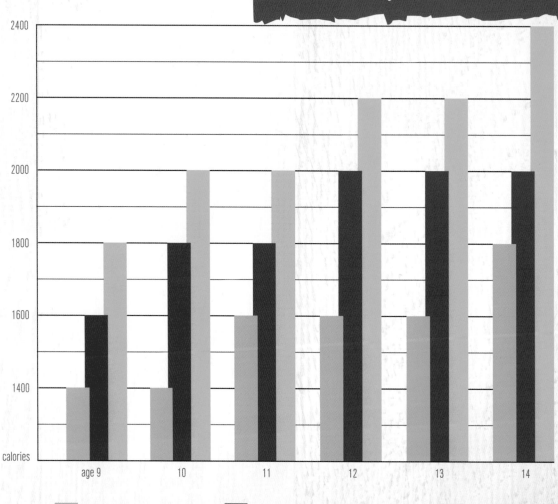

| | not active | moderately active | very active |

GIRLS VS BOYS

When it comes to exercise, experts recommend that children and adolescents get at least 60 minutes a day. But most aren't getting enough.

30 to 33% of boys aged between 11 and 15 are getting enough physical activity. But only. . .

24% of 11-year-old girls get enough exercise every day.

And by the age of 15, that percentage drops to

17%.

MORE EXERCISE?

Check this list for ideas – and the number of girls aged between 8 and 18 who took part in each activity last year.

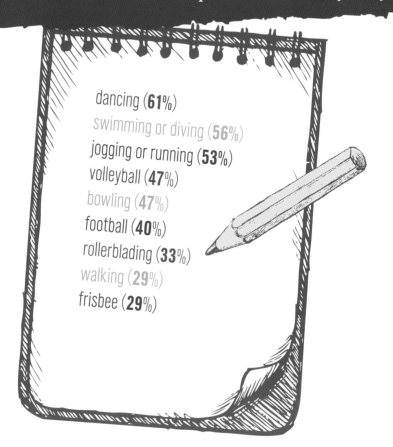

dancing (**61%**)
swimming or diving (**56%**)
jogging or running (**53%**)
volleyball (**47%**)
bowling (**47%**)
football (**40%**)
rollerblading (**33%**)
walking (**29%**)
frisbee (**29%**)

WORKOUT REMINDERS

- Don't eat within 1 hour before your workout. You might get cramps or feel sick.

- Drink water every 15 to 20 minutes while you work out, especially during hot weather. But don't gulp it! Take slow sips.

GETTING YOUR ZZZS

Sleep is like food for your body and brain. But many kids and teens aren't getting enough. Experts recommend at least **10 hours** a night for children and **9 to 10 hours** for teens. See who's getting their zzzs – and who isn't.

WHO GETS AT LEAST 9 HOURS A NIGHT?

The older you get, the more difficult it is to get the sleep you need. Why? During adolescence, your sleep patterns shift. Your body wants to stay awake longer at night and sleep in later in the morning.

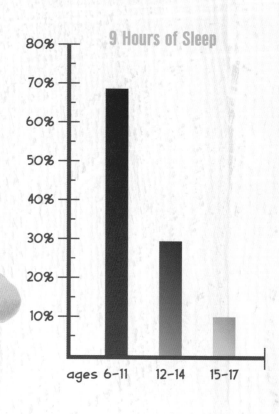

9 Hours of Sleep

ages 6–11   12–14   15–17

WHAT ELSE GETS IN THE WAY?

Lots of things interfere with a good night's sleep, but busy schedules and homework top the list. Here are the numbers of children and teens who can't sleep due to. . .

1. evening activities: **34%**
2. homework: **28%**
3. the temperature of the room (too hot or too cold): **18%**
4. noise in the house: **15%**
5. pets: **9%**

ELECTRONIC DEVICES? TURN 'EM OFF!

Leaving on devices like your TV, tablet or phone can interfere with sleep.

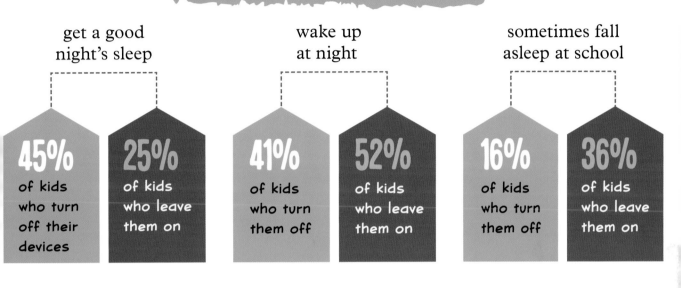

get a good night's sleep

45% of kids who turn off their devices

25% of kids who leave them on

wake up at night

41% of kids who turn them off

52% of kids who leave them on

sometimes fall asleep at school

16% of kids who turn them off

36% of kids who leave them on

1 more hour

That's how much extra sleep children and teens get each night if their parents enforce rules about bedtime.
Try to follow them – that extra hour is worth it!

3 WAYS TO UNWIND BEFORE BED

1. 30% of kids take a bath or shower

2. 24% listen to music

3. 21% read

BODY AND MIND

Your body and mind have a strong connection. If you explore the ways your body and mind work together, you'll feel more in control of both, especially as you head into your teenage years.

STRESSED OUT!

31%

of teens aged **13 to 17** say they feel more stressed than they did **a year ago.** And because of that stress . . .

36% feel more tired than usual.

30% of teens feel depressed or sad.

23% sometimes skip meals.

40%

of children report that they worry too much.

37%

23%

GIRLS VS BOYS

37% of teenage girls report feeling sad or depressed in the past month because of stress. Compare that to **23%** of teenage boys.

HOW DO TWEENS AND TEENS MANAGE STRESS?

■ tweens (aged 8 to 12)   ■ teens (aged 13 to 17)

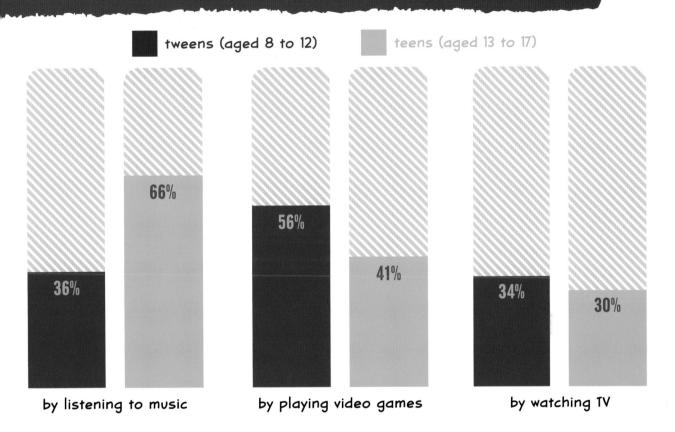

| by listening to music | by playing video games | by watching TV |

36%   66%   56%   41%   34%   30%

WHAT ELSE HELPS?

MOVING YOUR BODY!

After exercising. . .

- **53%** of teenagers say they feel good about themselves.
- **40%** say they're in a good mood.
- **32%** say they feel less stressed.

53%   40%   32%

HITTING THE SHEETS

1 in 5
teenagers say that when they don't get enough sleep, they're more stressed.

BODY TALK

Who do girls talk to when they're feeling stressed or have questions about their bodies? Most talk to friends or other girls their own age. Some talk to their parents, especially their mums. Others talk to a teacher, an aunt or another adult they trust.

83% — **83%** of teenagers say they have someone who is about their age that they trust and can confide in, such as a friend, sister or cousin.

15% — **15%** say they don't have someone like that in their lives.

78% — **78%** of teenagers say there's an adult other than a parent whom they can trust and confide in, such as a teacher, family friend or aunt.

21% — **21%** say they don't have another adult they confide in.

14-18 — **14- to 18-year-old** girls confide more in their parents than boys do – especially in their mums.

83% — **83%** of teenage girls said they write down their problems in a journal or diary.

6 TIPS FOR TALKING TO ADULTS

Being a teenager is exciting and sometimes confusing. It's easier to get through the confusing times if you have a trusted adult to talk to – someone who's been through what you're going through. But it's not always easy to feel comfortable talking to adult. These tips might make it easier.

1. **Start with small talk.** The more you practise talking – even about the small, silly stuff – the easier it'll be to talk about the big stuff.

2. **Pick the right time.** Make sure you have enough time to actually talk. Talk to a teacher after school instead of before. Talk to a parent while travelling in the car.

3. **Say what you need.** Just someone to listen to you? Or do you want advice? Be specific.

4. **Say what you feel.** If you're scared to talk about what's been going on with you or you are embarrassed to ask a question, say so!

5. **Take a break** if things get too heated. Come back to the conversation later, when you're feeling more calm.

6. **Keep talking.** The more you do, the easier it'll get. You'll work out your feelings, find answers to questions and feel more in control of your life – and your changing body.

Author bio

Erin Falligant has written more than 30 fiction and non-fiction books for children. Her advice books help tweens stand up to bullies, survive homework and embrace their changing bodies. Erin earned a Masters in Child Clinical Psychology and worked for more than 15 years as a children's book editor.

Books in this series:

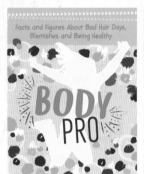

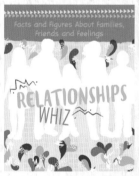